Drifter

poems by

Douglas Cole

Finishing Line Press
Georgetown, Kentucky

Other Books by Douglas Cole

The Cabin at the End of the World (Poetry)
The White Field (Novel)
The Blue Island (Poetry)
The Gold Tooth in the Crooked Smile of God (Poetry)
Bali Poems (Poetry)
The Dice Throwers (Poetry)
Western Dream (Poetry)
Interstate (Poetry)
Ghost (Novella)

Drifter

For Jenn

Copyright © 2025 by Douglas Cole
ISBN 979-8-88838-636-1 First Edition
All rights reserved under International and Pan-American Copyright Conventions. No part of this book may be reproduced in any manner whatsoever without written permission from the publisher, except in the case of brief quotations embodied in critical articles and reviews.

Publisher: Leah Huete de Maines
Editor: Christen Kincaid
Cover Art and Design: Douglas Cole
Author Photo: Jennifer Merritt

Order online: www.finishinglinepress.com
              also available on amazon.com

                    Author inquiries and mail orders:
                          Finishing Line Press
                              PO Box 1626
                      Georgetown, Kentucky 40324
                                    USA

Contents

Part I
Ghost Town

Preface 1
The Empty City 2
Spokane Falls at Dawn 3
The River 4
Snapshots at the Clinkerdagger Bar 5
The Grand Hotel 6
The Ridpath 7
The Disappearing Street 8
Epilogue 9

Part II
Drifting with Others

Derive, A Drift 13
Investigation of the Spectacle, Part One 15
Investigation of the Spectacle, Part Two 18
Empty Houses Ring 19
The West Door 21

Part III
DC Journal

DC on Entry 27
Dupont Circle 29
The Mortality of Film 30
Along These Lines 31
R Street 32
Dupont Circle South 33
Archaic Line 34
The Library of Headless Scholars 35
Place is the House of Being 36
Smoke and Mirrors 37
Cant of the Dead 38
Brocken's Specter at Shady Grove 39
Ouroboros 40

Capitol South 41
Metro Center 42
More Perfect Union 43
Found Art 44
Thomas Circle 45
Panorama 46
Nerve Center 48
Prelude to a Reckoning 50
Convergence 51
Babel 52
A Cold Clean Skeleton 53
Breaking the Roof 55
A Man Searching 56

Part IV
Cape Blanco Suite: The Dark Road Diaries

Progress 61
Midway on This Journey 62
No Answer 63
Umpqua 64
Reedsport 65
Cape Blanco 66
The Lighthouse Keeper 67
Morphic Zen in Oregon 68
Stuck in Medford 69
Revelation 70
Report 71
California Road 72
80 to the Bay 73
Looking through Time's Eye 74
Hallucination in a Rearview Mirror 75
Rivers 76
Roadside Sideshow 77
Let's Take This Moment to Consider 78
I Keep Looking for Myself 79

Part V
Eternal Return

The Divine City 83

*"...just got into town about an hour ago
took a look around see which way the wind blow..."*

From "Theory of the Dérive"

"One of the basic situationist practices is the *dérive* [literally: "drifting"], a technique of rapid passage through varied ambiances. Dérives involve playful-constructive behavior and awareness of psychogeographical effects, and are thus quite different from the classic notions of journey or stroll. In a dérive one or more persons during a certain period drop their relations, their work and leisure activities, and all their other usual motives for movement and action, and let themselves be drawn by the attractions of the terrain and the encounters they find there. Chance is a less important factor in this activity than one might think: from a dérive point of view cities have psychogeographical contours, with constant currents, fixed points and vortexes that strongly discourage entry into or exit from certain zones."

—Guy Debord, "Theory of the *Dérive*," *Situationist International Anthology*, Published by Bureau of Public Secrets, translated by Ken Knabb.

I

Ghost Town

"The primarily urban character of the dérive, in its element in the great industrially transformed cities—those centers of possibilities and meanings—could be expressed in Marx's phrase: 'Men can see nothing around them that is not their own image; everything speaks to them of themselves. Their very landscape is alive.'"
    —Guy Debord

Preface

This place is always post-war
river gulls circling wasted fields
gliding over anonymous windowsills
and Depression-era red brick hotels
overlooking the trainyard night

Enter this with an inland mind
the wind like theremin music
in a fifties version of the way
we imagine the end of the world—

a body beneath the radio tower
illuminated by a dime of light
streetlamps with no connections
gazing up at passing auroras
in the wonder of coming dawn

The Empty City

In the plaza on Howard Street you'll find the unlikely fountain
prohibited by iron rails beneath a walkway encased in bronze glass
and surrounded by would-be windows if the concept made it
through the financing, and tucked up in there like an afterthought
is Benjamin's Café with one woman serving through the afternoon,
her face a relief map of untreated tumors.

West on Main, Lincoln stands a mute copper witness to converging
afternoon drivers, and further west find the Shrine Auditorium with soot
black colonnades of Corinthian dolor and Sphinx replica with shattered
nose inglorious on a side street without even the embrace of a desert.

Into Peaceful Valley and Glovers Field a young woman carries a baby
and leaves a trail of milk blankets on the street of abandoned homes
begun in the dream of the nearby river with shopping carts in empty lots
and cars that will never run all there in the old woman's gaze as she sits
on porch under tides of afternoon clouds blowing over—and is that
the howl of water below or the sigh of traffic on the bridge above?

Ascend the steel steps through green hillside artifacts:
whiskey bottle, lost coat, papers, the coded cry of graffiti,
turn and see one child running through a relay of barking dogs.
Soon enough the streets empty, not one sound but the river,
construction begun and ended midway in rubble and oily pools,
one engine in the train yard going nowhere, all in all, born old
and driving their carts over the bones of the dead among ghostly
whispers of the spirits looking for a way back in.

Spokane Falls at Dawn

I

You might envision the future like this, streets devoid of people,
a little wind, the hints of something that could have been,
the form of a person emerging from nothing more than paper
with date unknown, photographs of an earlier age,
mannequins in white clothes faded by time, and you calling
with no answer coming but the sway of suspension bridge,
river rushing through black monolithic rock as you search.

II

A howl coming out of the water, and you realize
a whole cascade of voices woven in the current,
the way your cry joins that traffic of wind
funneling through the alleyways and torn awnings
down to the train yard, the gulley, the alluvial wash
where we raise another crucifix out of the dust.

The River

Not a soul among the empty rides, Ferris wheel, plastic pig,
and teacup archway to the river—

No one in the streets or on the grass banks carved
meticulously into true red earth and the river—

Power plant windows and suspension bridge,
white water colliding at high rage of the river—

South Cedar Street, roar of vehicles, barking dogs,
the worker heading home who knows but rarely thinks
about the voices and the constant chorus of the river—

Snapshots in the Clinkerdagger Bar

Bill—A flabby social-groping sot, brown-nose
state bureaucrat humping the American dollar.

Betty—though she claims the totem of the bear, I see
more bovine behavior, as though I actually stood
beside a cow quietly farting and ruminating in a field.

Larry—from his eyes you see one poised so perilously
on the edge of a great vortex, terror he nightly invents,
fighting against the comforts of a black sea of dreams.

Marlene—smart by nature, mind geared-up like a mighty blade
in the sawmill of the world's ideas, yet, curiously easily bored
and unsure if anyone really buys her various incarnations.

Tina—plays a version of a self while real self leers
from its morbid-child, moth-smothered cave—
personality carved from a parade of ghosts.

The Grand Hotel

Some rooms must be haunted the way Davenport sits
bronze at the east end of the lobby, the way the fish
circle dumb and bug-eyed in the central fountain,
and faces in the corridor photographs communicate
their lives through the holy gray emulsion's fade,
the way our shadows walk the Escher courtyards,
climbing mushroom stairs, in love, beautifully in love.

The Ridpath

Miners, farmers, conventioneers and train yard bulls,
freeways, hills, pools in the middle of Astroturf,
spies, detectives, students and drunks, soon, soon
the building sinks, bell-hops and clerks dissolve,
the maids with no English vanish through the walls—
everything else is gutted: wires, pipes, carpet scraps,
the hotel taking on the unruly shape of the city below.

The Disappearing Street

They just got through filming the new medical series.
It's supposed to be a good one with A-listers in it
and some locals. They filmed scenes in the Cunningham house,
got a shot of Ryan with their daughter who takes classes at Gonzaga.
She's studying literature and wants to be a teacher.
Everyone hopes she'll come back here to live when she's done.

Epilogue

We went to the fair in '74, he said.
It was the last time my father was with us
before disappearing into the Saint James Apartments.
He left everything he owned behind—
paintings, clothes, power tools in the basement.
He was fired up to see the expo, so we drove out
in a wood-panel station wagon to the World's Fair.
I'd never felt that kind of heat before: the road
crackling in the desert rest stop, the buzz of crickets,
the snakes sliding through the pine needles.
When we got there, the rides were rickety bone-shakers,
and exhibits of the future already looked like the past,
but I don't remember seeing the river.
Of all things, the river. Funny I'd forget that.
It cuts right through the city.

II

Drifting with Others

"One can dérive alone, but all indications are that the most fruitful numerical arrangement consists of several small groups of two or three people who have reached the same level of awareness."
—Guy Debord

Derive, a Drift

(Wednesday, June 4, with Chien-Chih Huang, a Buddhist Nun)

If you strike the handles in the north stairwell of the college some of them make music, a kind of low drumbeat or heartbeat, and already we can smell the smokers even before we push through the door into the courtyard where we find on the condemned wall of the portable the words: AODUREM! or something like that, in the script of the urban paint poets, there beside the terracotta sun face hanging on the chain link fence which is also part of the condemned circumscription that says this will not last much longer, look now, take what you will.

The Howel street neighborhood society has adorned the sidewalk with roses, and look down near the roots and you'll see two rusted railroad spikes and a broken winch, placed there with intention, arranged for a very few who will ever see, who will only see if they wonder who chose these objects and said rise from decay and be part of the crumbled wall that holds these flowers in place: resurrection, love that asks for nothing, an offering if you're blessed to see it.

The wind is calm and warm and the tags on the lamppost are the only marks left of someone's passage, and look up there you'll see a rusted fairy with a star wand on the apartment patio that will by noon be awash in sunlight, but don't miss the abandoned or stolen and tossed aside leather briefcase, nearly brand new, empty, maybe ransacked, someone's lost object with a calculator left beside it because no one steals math.

Stop! because a truck blocks the sidewalk and the panels are locked (I checked them) and yes this is a form of repulsion but only for a moment because nothing stops this flow or the sway of the tennis shoes hanging from the power lines over the intersection, yet among the immaculate trees and shrubs of The Place Apartments we find a plant stripped from its pot left to dry up and die, so I take it because "saving" is now part of the theme of this drift.

More shoes and graffiti say "I was here" as we pass the Abonita Apartments where only the resident or the resident-friend can find passage through the Entraguard, but a string of three Chihuahuas converge on us as one last domestic visitation before we cross Broadway and the street plate with one word on it: "Common," as if to say, there, behold the empty Godfather's Pizza that has remained empty and for lease this last year and is slowly fading into one of those burned out spots in the city that take on the look of a haunted face and no one even sees it.

The reservoir, and who would have thought that water would ever be a target, vulnerable, and if you think about it we do that to ourselves; although, it does reside next to the funeral home and let's hope that the furnaces are at peak temperature and that even then what floats out and over that water means no harm even to this sad sleeper in the grass or the Abyssinian in the window, and behold the gate to the reservoir is open, though the signs say "No Trespass," so we enter, waved at fiercely by the orange vest too far away to stop us now, and we descend the newly graded slope as if into a cathedral.

Near the ball field where stragglers have encamped, one man has not only a space heater but a television set plugged into the lamppost (I didn't know lampposts had outlets), arranging his things, shaking out a blanket, as the small family cuddled up to the bleachers offer their bread to a stranger while one shoots-up in the leg.

Andy Kaufman on a telephone pole, still trying to come back from the dead or climb out of a Bartell's shopping cart and through the iron hinges of the German United Church of Christ (Vereinigte Deutschspachige Kirche), where a robin hops onto the fence and a car alarm begins to blare, church after church of worship, and as if given (for this is a walk of resurrections), we come upon a pot and soil, a perfect home for our found plant.

Investigation of the Spectacle

(Friday, April 23rd 4:00 pm-2:00am with JW)

"*Our loose lifestyle and even certain amusements considered dubious that have always been enjoyed among our entourage—slipping by night into houses undergoing demolition, hitchhiking nonstop and without destination through Paris during a transportation strike in the name of adding to the confusion, wandering in subterranean catacombs forbidden to the public, etc.—are expressions of a more general sensibility which is no different from that of the dérive.*"
—Guy Debord

Part 1

    We begin at Machiavelli's, hearth of autumn, essential rays last falling into the depths of the city. Our mission is not a drunken pub-crawl, per se, but examination of all possibilities, the flesh parade, the Friday night flow of Seattle…show us what you're made of. But Machiavelli's is prohibitively crowded with suit shades erect before martinis like flowers with the look of being looked at and faces made to meet faces; hence, artifice and congestion sucking time (waiting for JW as he extricates himself from miasmic forces…I hold no judgments.) I am thinking last night of summer, with beauty quiet sun through the windows, as the Space Needle shimmers in its future to the west.
    From Machiavelli's we drop into the Baltic room, set-up in progress for urban jungle fusion, where we have a scotch and begin the process by dissecting the work world so as to leave it behind…green succubae and rosy imps, clowns and conservatives, minute hoarders and punctuationists… long live bad spellers and have another drink. Our destination? Vague notions unspoken in order not to neck-tie our flow…food being partial need and goal…where we find ourselves is where we are welcome. Step out streetwise, and a young woman jumps out of a car to meet a friend, her artificially red hair aglow in the last-light…tarnished mirrors that gaze… yet, who can say this isn't beautiful?
    "What is this dérive, exactly," JW asks me.
    "Well, literally a drift through the landscape aware of what you encounter as psychogeography…a representation of minds that create and inhabit and shape it as it is, becoming aware of the layers, conscious of your reactions to objects and buildings and the spirits that invest them, letting yourself be drawn, aware of what attracts you or repels you or what prohibits you from moving through a space or what you ignore because of

some gravitational pull so strong you'd violate any law or ownership that would otherwise stop you… or something like that."

Down Pine Street past the new hotel with bronze sculpture shaped like a crumpled piece of paper…beauty? "That's just the kind of art that leaves me cold," JW says, "that kind of orange I-beam art…" Henry Moore had been badly imitated, but I'm sure it cost a lot of money. Red Circle on White? Yellow Lines Number 50? Beauty? The abstract doesn't connect the dots this evening; we want the organic explosion, the sacred truth of old.

And JW keeps stopping on empty streets while I keep on walking. There's a haptic quality in reacting to a stoplight. From a kaleidoscope equipped with consciousness we're drilled by the funfair into workers coordinating with machines.

"Potentially we could get a ticket," he says.

"That's anti-dérive talking."

"Anti-dérive?"

"Shock. Like the first encounter."

"Can you imagine seeing a city for the first time? The fear, the horror of crowds for the first time?"

"It would take some adapting, some going to sleep. The dérive is like waking up."

We walk through the intersection and see a sheriff's car across the street, but there's someone just ahead of us jaywalking, and I say, "Who do you think will get a ticket?"

Now JW's in flow, and I have to reign him back when he nearly steps in front of a moving car. He's done the same for me in the past… we owe each other our lives. And as a woman is cleaning up and shutting down the flower shop on the corner of First and Pike, I step in and ask if she has any Passion Flowers. No, but she gives me a card and tells me to call the manager…he can get anything. I've got plans for that Passion Flower.

We slide down Post Alley…food, not yet…another drink first as we slip into the Alibi Room where, I believe, our dérive begins in earnest: the beautiful people as couples and groups at candle-lit tables. The hostess is richly tattooed with Celtic floral patterns on her arms and neck and eyebrows…does she have a Passion Flower? I check her wrists. "Say, do you know the other hostess who used to work here? She had the black lines tattooed on her shoulder for good years, red lines for the bad?"

"That's Adrianne. She still works here."

"Ah…"

"I don't know if I would want those reminders…" JW says.

We step over to the bar.

"So is what you've described the essence of dérive as you've learned it, or is it your own take?"

"I just make it up as I go."

"So, what makes this a space people are drawn to?"

We look around. "It has a view, but not much of one," JW says. "It has comedic brick walls, it's pretty small, closed in…"

"It's remote, obscure, hidden…it provides an element of discovery. Or you have to know about it, like belonging to a secret society. Essentially, grotto chic."

Outside the Alibi room is the gum wall, next to the haunted theater, and along the wall, people have impressed their chewed gum into a constellation of gum explosions. Some have pennies stuck to them. Some are shaped like faces with burnt cigarettes sticking out of them. Some are stretched out into star patterns, nebulae, clouds and one a flute-playing Kokopelli. This array spreads upwards about ten feet and along a two-hundred-foot stretch of wall. People are standing around, smoking, looking at it, adding to it. JW and I stop, draw in close, examine it. It is beautiful. "People's DNA," JW says. "Yet, you wouldn't want to touch it."

"Creates its own preservative sheen…"

"That one looks fresh."

Further down the alleyway, past the razor wire tulips (to prevent people from climbing over and jumping off…it's about a forty-foot drop… ultimate anti-dérive), we enter a newly updated span of Post Alley. It has the immaculate polish of a German Transplatz: polished tiles, clean glass brightly shimmering, and yet the feeling I get is that if you stay too long you'll be hit by a vaporizing ray coming down from a high pillbox slit in the grey cement. Unlike the gum wall which creates both an attraction and a repulsion, I want to move on quickly from here. This space is cold and sterile, and looking up, what do we see? Orange I-beams exploding from the walls.

Part 2

    The Trattoria in Pioneer Square occupies a corner with large windows that frame the life of the street flowing by. The evening like a scar seems to thicken. The cafe is nearly empty now (10 o'clock), with a man and a woman sitting in a corner, the lightning of their souls extending in the colors of a newly formed love. We sit at the bar counter and lean in like nighthawks. "It has the ambiance of a Fifties diner," JW says, and sure enough the case behind the bar is full of pies and ketchup bottles.

    Food, glorious food…funereal appetite, every bite is sacred. Fortified, we head back out to the street with no destination other than south. We continue down First Avenue until we end up at a goofy western bar with an electronic bull and pool tables and air saturated with night pleasures vainly sported. It's loaded with women in miniskirts and lycra tank-tops and jar-headed guys in jeans and muscle shirts. Perfect. There is a line, and we wait a few moments while a couple of guys get into a fight, but they're too drunk to do any damage. One of them gets hauled off by his girlfriend, stumbling full of threats into the darkness.

    Inside, we crowd surf to the bar where a woman falls against me, drunk, and I literally hold her up and say, "Are you all right?" She sort of laughs, sort of speaks, but she is basically incoherent at this point. Then some of her 'friends' come and take her away. Fair forward traveler.

    The women who tend the bar get up on the counter and dance in a line. They've got a little routine they do. The music is so loud that we can't talk. We just move and drink and observe. A big guy stone drunk orders a drink at the bar and the girl takes his head and places it between her knees and pours the alcohol directly down his gullet and shakes his head violently with her thighs and pushes him back into the crowd as he swallows down the froth of her ire. He leers and lurches and sweats and opens his mouth and the people part religiously before him.

    Not much to sum up here. It's all alcohol and sex and the resuscitation of dead minutes, hope and thrills and something to remember beyond sleep and laundry and the jobs that eat us alive. Climb on the bull and ride, the saddle polished to a gleam by a million pelvic dreams. Climb on the bull and slide right off. Moment in a lifetime, lifetime in a moment. I find an old gumball machine and punch a few coins into it. I win a little gold ring with a blue stone held by tiny metal claws. I drop it into the tip bucket on the way out and the hostess grabs it up and puts it on her finger and shows it around like she just got engaged.

Empty Houses Ring

(Sunday, May 16, alone...)

"The maximum area of this spatial field does not extend beyond the entirety of a large city and its suburbs. At its minimum it can be limited to a small self-contained ambiance: a single neighborhood or even a single block of houses if it's interesting enough (the extreme case being a static-dérive of an entire day within the Saint-Lazare train station)."
　—Guy Debord

in the open house, for sale by owner, my mind floats through doorways and the sad little divider that says this is entry and over there stark living room in immaculate disguise and straight ahead is bathroom polished to regal gleam with floral lamp covers and chrome towel rods like exposed and intricate machine parts, ah...

while beyond is an old man bent to garden beside his checkerboard lawn, years of time-fade on his shoulders, tending under gaze of cats between one roofless tarp-covered house and a moss-bound garage with gnomes singing, always be drunk, drunk as a consul, drunk as a variable hatter in the outer urban zone, especially on Marshall Street...

descending through the green canal of 48th Street, over-bowered by maple trees and blackberries, with a "Don't dump on Seattle" sign, I find a well-worn little mystery trail I follow like a white rabbit-ass when I come upon a thick vine to which someone has duct-taped a wine bottle, a swing dangling from the grand escape ladder...

emerging into one junk-filled yard where every space is laden with boards and tires and tubes and appliances and a van undriveable loaded like a mind in tatters...

as Lowman Beach opens with its trinity trees calling come come be by the waters, where families poke around on the temporary spit shaped like a question mark, dog barking at the waves, and the man in his wife's dress stands on the stone ledge dreaming her back from the dead, keeping her alive by wig and mascara and majorette baton with the long sad expression of so much time left ahead...

in through the driftwood cove and what was once a dock pile, what was once a ship hull, what was once a buoy, what was once, what was once...all awash in the waves at my feet...

climbing the hillside into Lincoln Park, sliding on the dirt slope, using roots as ropes, I see the land scars, how looking down is looking back is perilous in the silver flare of the water lacking moon and glitter, ancient mother trees rising from the sea and reaching for the sky, so much the way the eye lures us towards what we see and what we imagine…

back on Fauntleroy an explosion of cars and the Kenney Home with faces in windows looking out like deportees gazing back on lands to which they'll never return, perfect grass edged to the precision of a knife blade and pansies exquisitely worried with inflection and formaldehyde dolor, and beyond the horseshoe driveway the wind vein always points south…

in the schoolyard where a child shoots hoops with his shadow through a netless rim some glory breaks through, but to hope is to hope for the wrong thing, and California Street won't ratchet up the sunlight to more than intermittent radiance, shops and bars in slow Sunday paper page-turning time-fade, café soundtrack voice singing we are all lost in space…

as real estate agents collect their sign boards and dogs flop on porches and in spite of mold growing inside the plastic garden cover behind the teriyaki shop say yes, say yes, yes in a dirge in a chorus of wind chimes, yes, we are music, and yes this same sad song plays when time this generation shall waste and these lawns and windows and brief timid blossoms blow on and all things even horrible turn to grace…

The West Door

(May 21st)

"The human mind is an active originator of experience rather than just a passive recipient of perception."
—Immanuel Kant

1st Station:
This begins and ends with one vision: a girl, maybe 16 or 17, sitting in a chair, a sky-blue blanket wrapped around her, suitcases, boxes, and a few pieces of furniture lined up along the sidewalk. Behold your Queen.

2nd Station
The city feels cold today. I am on my own, not one soul out here to break this solitude, ecstasy out of reach. I wander over to the corner market, buy cigarettes, give two away, the guy with a face etched down to golgothic shards tells me, "You can get those for three and a quarter in Burien."
    I light—"Yeah, but I'd have to go to Burien."

3rd Station
This thought reverberates from the institution corridors: a lingering misconception that exposes another problem I hear as two people pass, which I seem to have heard many times, "How can I be of use to anyone when I am such a mess?" An ancient conversation still going on, an answer in the walls that comes: "That is when you are most called upon to give."

4th Station
Love Vivace, but cell phones, lunch dates, books and big ideas can't fill the vacancy. It's because of what "I am." A crowd of stars, laments, shadows we carry through the sunless day. Such are the stranger things…a sine reflecting on the ceiling, a cosine in the darker strings. Remember water shimmering in the reservoir? The core of many hearts laid bare.

5th Station
At 11th and John there's a maple tree so large that to stand beneath it is to stand essentially within it, its black arms hanging down, and you cannot see its entirety. As Paul Tillich writes, "The sign-event which gives the mystery of revelation does not destroy the rational structure of the reality in which it appears." Which is to say that this tree stands here, at the moment I perceive it, the tree of knowledge that is not knowable in its entirety…can't know everything…which is to say that I stepped into the moment recalling

"The Blue Bouquet" when the character, "I," looks up and beholding the stars thinks, "…the universe was a vast system of signs, a conversation between giant beings. My actions, the cricket's saw, the star's blink, were nothing but pauses and syllables, scattered phrases from that dialogue."

6th Station
The young man at Victrola moves in a mercurial field from one end of the counter to the other and back again, and when he sees me, he leaps over and looks me in the eye. And he who welcomes you welcomes me…. Nervosa. Full of Energy. And I say, "I'm in no hurry." In a single moment it is impossible to see him entirely.

7th Station
Two students of mine and a newer stranger are sitting under the gun art. They are studying human trafficking. Woes and conflict. I look at their faces. What words have passed between them? When I go to the tables outside to have my coffee, I read in Paul Auster's *The Invention of Solitude*:

> One sees nothing but one's own thoughts…A voice speaks, a woman's voice speaks, a voice that speaks stories of life and death, has the power to give life… There is also the equal and opposite temptation to look at the world as though it were an extension of the imaginary.

8th Station:
Branching into Spiderwoman, in another tongue, where the Diyin Dine'e spoke the world into being. Leslie Marmon Silko writes:

> Thought-Woman, the spider,
> named things and
> as she named them
> they appeared.
> She is sitting in her room
> thinking of a story now
> I'm telling you the story
> she is thinking.

9th Station
This used to be Presbyterian, I believe, but now it is called All Pilgrims Christian Church, blackened bricks still warm to the touch. A few drifters are crouched in the back, casting lots. In the courtyard there is a stone sculpture of perpetual water flowing that resembles the sculpture at Saint Ignatius of our Lady and the Perpetual Milk of Love and Mercy…bars, however, keep me out…Wright's "St. Judas":

> Banished from heaven, I found this victim beaten,
> Stripped, kneed, and left to cry. Dropping my rope
> Aside, I ran, ignored the uniforms:
> Then I remembered bread my flesh had eaten,
> The kiss that ate my flesh.

10th Station
Back on Broadway, in front of the church, I give Nancy my change. She's hanging out, panhandling, holding a spot on the sidewalk, free to talk, and she says, "Yeah, they used to camp out down there," pointing down the slope on the west side of the church, "build fires and stuff. I guess that's why the church put up the bars."
"Looks like an old church."
"It is."
"Real bells in the tower," I say, pointing at the ropes.
"You know, I've never heard them ring."

11th Station
The new library does not have a marked section for poetry. I inquire about this from the woman with doughy flesh and shaking hands, dear spirit (the kind of woman who arranges coffee and cookies for the social hour after church) devoted to helping you find something, even if she doesn't have it, so slow, so thorough, so…I run into Kelly, strange kid, wide-eyes that never blink, mechanical twitches, who follows me into the stacks where I find the half-shelf of poetry they do have, and he says, "I like to chronologize my experiences." I take down a book. He wrote his thesis on LSD, the thirst for knowledge.

12th Station
On Boylston, their possessions lined up in stacks along the sidewalk: couch, tables, boxes, suitcases, and the one girl in a chair, a blue blanket wrapped around her. All I do is stop, and she tells me they were evicted. Her roommates didn't tell her they hadn't paid rent since December. Her name is Renee, left behind by the voice of the winds, la lumiere des coincidence. She asks me for a cigarette, and I give her three. She has a swollen cheek from an abscessed tooth. She is waiting for a friend to come, smoking, her legs curled up, the blanket sculpting her into the shape of divine desolation, mistress of the universe full of grace. Our lady of perpetual sorrows, succor, hope, pray for us now and at the hour of our death…

III

DC Journal

"A dérive often takes place within a deliberately limited period of a few hours, or even fortuitously during fairly brief moments; or it may last for several days without interruption. In spite of the cessations imposed by the need for sleep, certain dérives of a sufficient intensity have been sustained for three or four days, or even longer. It is true that in the case of a series of dérives over a rather long period of time it is almost impossible to determine precisely when the state of mind peculiar to one dérive gives way to that of another. One sequence of dérives was pursued without notable interruption for around two months. Such an experience gives rise to new objective conditions of behavior that bring about the disappearance of a good number of the old ones…"
—Guy Debord

DC on Entry

O capitol of shade! Twin mirror!
Over the Department of Education,
tacked on, banners in red and black
letters say, "No Child Left Behind,"
as temporary as a dictatorship.

Circular sandstone pueblo-style
Native American museum,
yet note that you do not
leave the way you came in.
So this is no kiva, and the
journey through is no ceremony.

Sacred geometry as thesis
writ in the sculpture outside
the flight museum.

Archives building—"The ties
that bind the lives of our people…"
—clutching the collective past,
knowing without "understanding,"
(cf Aldous Huxley), warehouse of
documents crumbling until
re-preserved by the host
of memorticians wandering
labyrinths reciting scriptures.

The early colony:
grim fundamental community,
cowering stance towards god—so,
we shouldn't be surprised when
the head rises from time to time
to throw its judgmental glare
across the nation.

The slats and black granite
of the J. Edgar Hoover building
with clean dread sidewalks
hooked directly into every
surveillance eye in the city,
watchful camera, homeland dreams.

The Treasury—right hand
gob for the White House—
with old folks riding the blue
busses through the soldier
statues or wandering in circles
on the pathway webs that match
the design of a Confederate flag.

Names on buildings in over-script,
yet the department of commerce
looks more like an old dollar bill
after inflation. What are all these
blind people looking at?

City of monuments,
city conceived,
give us a vision beyond
the filthy Potomac
and floating carcasses,
yea, I anoint myself
with your disease.

They begin like the first
slow movements of a black
river rising ankle deep,
and you see yourself
and those around you
reflected in your own gaze
among names, the great wall
of names as you descend.

Lincoln enclosed
in his marble temple,
58 steps ascending
(the years he lived)
like atomic plates
to the statue's feet
and out goes a silent cry
across the savage mall
beneath his stony gaze.

Dupont Circle

Bars and chains and exploded roses
boys of Rocksboro and the Grenadian embassy
taking their turtles for walks in the arcade
old redbrick stoops of hope and hopelessness
the Carlyle Hotel with black and white tiles
and the Nigerian clerk on graveyard shift
floating empty hours under a torn speaker
with Sinatra crooning the cold iron night

The Mortality of Film

Unreal hallways, tunnels, lightless passing bodies,
machines humming in rooms, faded archives,
yellow manuscripts, broadsides, records of the dead
and the newly born, film reels turning to vinegar,
voices, faces, landscapes in a panoramic gasp
tumbling into canvas bins loaded with hollow canisters,
hunched up rootless scholars with little check-out slips,
dramas running through ratchet teeth that eat you alive
in darkrooms under the big clock of correspondences
sinking earthwise through great seas of dreaming,
doorway opening like a film cell blossoming gold,
potent balm burning away on a hot projector light.

Along These Lines

Here was a road once.
The ones who traveled it knew
to get lost in spiderweb streets,
trees with haunting vine ropes,
and each rotunda offers up
its own well-lit hallucinations:
horses bending into buck knives,
irreparable gnawing teeth
that vanish as we pass through
the scaffolding like allegories.
In the amniotic sunset hour,
the brow slants over courtyards
where we can see everything
in its anatomic refinement,
and nothing can touch us.

R Street

Rising and rolling cardinal calls,
rats scuttling into the ivy
under colonnades of sandstone
and the black iron gates,
shelters of cold war terror
and snapshot gunfire streets,
coughing carnival of inveterate
weed smokers we pass
with laughing clouds swirling
and evaporating in every step.

Dupont Circle South

Where'd he get the purple tie?
He bums a cigarette off me
but can't get it lit with my lighter
while these show-tune kids sidle by,
drama on their cell phones,
and the fountain drools into its pool,
with naked bodies in the grass,
near-accidents every few minutes
in the chaos lanes, horns and brakes.
Sometimes I say divinity walks in rags.
Sometimes the dream in stone
slides right into my soul.
Sometimes I hear someone say,
where's the illuminating lightning,
the big annihilating strike?

Archaic Line

I've got a few more questions
no book is going to answer,
here where no one talks except to say,
"Larry didn't kill the rabbit, Eileen did."
"Time to pray, hear and obey,"
as garbage trucks haul last night away,
smash compacting dining sets, cribs,
the heaps from which we're made,
dusky interiors of strange disease
under shadows of wine-dark eaves.
Who among you remembers
the kiss that brought us here?
Luxurious moment crawling free,
wet realization of a dream and flight
and the cool calculous involved in
signing a declaration of Independence?

The Library of Headless Scholars

Reading room statues with great eyes
that see nothing, books shuffled out
on conveyor belts, pneumatic tubes
coughing up rolled papers in triplicate.
Where is our poet laureate?
Where is the soul of the institution?
Shades come and sit beside you
as you pour over the solar glories
between the pages yellow with age
in the nerve center, the nation's brain,
whispering, turn the page, turn the page.

Place is the House of Being

We arrive in flesh machines
and walk among crowds unseen
while in the back of the mind
god's finger stirs a pool of dreams

heads bent over brittle pages
squint print words words words
from which the world is made

slide into the catacomb
seek the great vision
kiva sweat lodge great cathedral
archive shrine divine altar
scribblers who take us to the center

Smoke and Mirrors

Hallowed glass, light,
the great American Bird,
arrows and stars, the luminaries—
none of it compares to the soft
blue marbled veins in your wrist.

Cant of the dead,
monument field,
like an old Hollywood
end of the world movie
with brains on fire—

political art.

Brocken's Specter at Shady Grove

Stuck in the Takoma station
with buzzing flies, mosquitoes, crickets,
moth vain punching at a platform light,
nothing moving nothing.

The train arrives with no destination,
eyes flicker in tunnels, birdlike faces,
as if we awoke at the bottom of a well,
swimming up through boiling night.

Ouroboros

A demon is fidgeting beside me
in the colonies, among the corridors,
with books of stone terminal weight,
like a monk praying inside his bones.

Scholars with dust on their glasses
squint like pensive cattle in elite type
at the dark map of the card catalogue,
their thumb smudges on the paper,
eyes like holes, clutch-stain of dead hands.

Robert Fludd put it all together
under one grand mosaic philosophy.
I understand it while I write it out
but keep smelling the plague years
on my hands as I leave the building.

Beaver mask and marble scrolls,
lifting a head from paving stones
transforming into isles of geometry,
I wander streets infant dreamed.

Capitol South

Monumental seething offices
incandescent doorways

the last train of the night
with musician playing alone
on the concourse edge

we feel our way like blind moles

not one straight street
to encode this wild connection

while lightning angels slouch
like laundry in fluorescent halos
over skeletons of wreckage

Melmoth makes a clean escape

Metro Center

Laughter at the M station, then sirens,
shooting in the murder capital of the universe.

The crowds disperses, nothing but a stain.

In the window, a hand holds back a curtain,
one face then another just over the shoulder.

More Perfect Union

Broken glass and rafters of apartment rooms,
mad dawn muttering like fleur de lyse bums
come to beg cigarettes and spare change,
crazy masons conjuring holy trees of science,
sunset streaks of firefly light, sigh of the Potomac,
overwhelming shadows from the Valley of the Kings,
moonlight glittering on Liberty Athena Minerva,
darling of inspiration, and who's here at my right
still nodding off in the sundry fetid tiger canal,
while no-nothings hurl a popestone into the well,
for the machine, the great machine of days over 100,
with slow horse in the millyard, beer stein of amber fizz,
cold river spit with the unseen bullfrogs of the mere
at center and circumference of this line of beauty.

Found Art

Mad ranting subway
host in retreating light
and avenues of confusion
dirt and dust

You left your manifesto
on the sidewalk
with anger scribblings
and hunger quotes
of meaningless connections

and my favorite is
the cross heart
silver mother spirit
cloud conquistadora
here in many forms
among us passing
through secret gardens

Wonder revealing
the serpent soft sacred
nest and membrane as
the cool electric phantom
palm tree sways

Thomas Circle

Rain wet black streets,
headlights, senatorial shades…
everything familiar, as though
another self never left.

A monument to…
I don't know…admire
marble and granite,
the memory of Europe,
an empty stage…
the smell of damp overcoats
and eyes like stones.

At night in the hotel room,
I hear strangers fighting,
television gunfire,
children running in the halls,
waiting for a dream
to override this fantasy.

Let the process unfold,
get on with the disease.
I can already tell
I'll be the fool of this group.
Which of my charades
will I parade today?

Here come the great clouds,
here comes the mad minuet
storm of hungry ants in
time-lapse collapsing the body
to its black canopy foliage
but oh—

this empire rolls
like a sea, like a swell,
old man muttering answers
here in the circle…maybe,
perhaps we'll meet again,
but for now, farewell.

Panorama

Out-of-towner cowboy rocking on
his boot-heels in the train sway,
silver suits, mesmerizing anonymity—
transfer tokens for expired rides,
pockets full of currency I can't convert

as I walk through the unbound field.

Louis the XVI and Marie Antoinette
step lightly and watch for blood.
The omphalos opens. Up rise the rats,
up rise the gutter men earth anointed
and the travelers from the old country
forgetting with every step…

welcome to the spectacle…
trying to embrace a cloud,
nothing you'd ever known before,
now a stranger behind the window
whispering in your ear, go, so gently…
the mouth of heaven, door of the abyss,
bewildered mother bathing
her child in the television glow of
another assassination, another war…

Who will build the need fires?
Who remembers the hymns?

Paris, London, New York, Berlin,
El Dorado, voyage of discovery…
subterranean cinemas unreeling
a canvas door behind the screen…
N-dimensional, halo-essence, echo
explosion descending a spiral staircase,
the moon spider loom-weaving
the village girl's hands and city streets,
with the multivocative idiot son
barking in the basement…

Life Magazine washes up on rocks,
open to immaculate Cadillac
driven by starlet in green glasses, red scarf...
she is waving from eternity...Hollywood
plants its seed, late-night infection,
the future child stirring in the womb
long after this world is gone...

as I walk the unbound field,

brother stranger other self in room above
long ago and yet to come, that spark,
that war of atoms at the heart of the sun...

    Volaré,

with legions arriving, clowns, calliope music.

Nerve Center

Holy auburn wood, hands that ever felt,
a sea anemone with tendrils reaching out
through a reading lamp on Sunday afternoon.

Off to the side hear the old one singing…

*Sometimes I feel,
like a motherless child….*

Here at place 135 with an October cold
and a mind like a fuzzy hammer,
spirit of the field, grand insight will come,
wet city night, and wind like a merciless knife
cutting the eyes, the bones…for a moment,
revelation 135, firmament, the ultimate stagecraft.
Sit in this chair if you don't believe me,
touch the brass plate with psychomimetic intensity,
and behold, She will open.

Italian marble draws you into
the epic or the patricide:
blame M. Boyer, he can handle it,
a Lewis Carol dream in echo…
Ohio set right down in front of us,
really, your ass is O—Hi—O.
Ah, love your kids, your sad ongoing
dream-intruding voice, blinkless eyes.
I'm just an October head-cold.

Rant…rant and rave, the lost domain,
the little blue cousin of corruption
showing in the works, insidious intent.
Pick a scab till it bleeds warring tonalities.
You belong to wind fragments therein.
And all you have to do is ask…
Rome with all the bickering, going fast…

"How is it possible for us earthly creatures,
or rather divine Images, howsed and obscured

in clayie tabernacles, to wade, of ourselves,
through the confused labyrinth of the creature,
unto the bright Essence of the creator?"
In Robert Fludd, Mosaicall Philosophy i…

The suicide in alphabet city—which are you?
Come on, Octavio, tell us another story,
not about big regimes or the sinking ship,
we've heard those before, we've lived those
ambiguities long enough—give us the sacred.
We've journeyed far to know what we are,
so break the tableaux, the only death—

Robert Fludd, Mosaicall Philosophy i:
"By penetrating with mental speculation
and operative perfection into the earthly
Circumference or mansion thereof,
and so dive, or attain by little and little
unto the heavenly Palace."

Who remembers the hymns?
Swirling marble watery thoughts?
Let this book be a testament to our escape.
At space 135, Alcove 2, Supplemento MRR ALU
AE 61.E6 1979/80, Page 433, kingdom of heaven.
The handiwork showeth…

"Los acontecimientos registrados en 1979
convirtieron a este pais en escenario
de todo genero de violencias
con un balance de numerosos muertos…"

The golden thread…

Prelude to a Reckoning:

Life in installments, fit-thoughts,
and your eyes as bright as water:
same old garbage trucks at work,
same old conversations taken up,
that feeling something's going on
dispelled on arrival but in the cool
air a sense of impending storm…

Convergence

Kaleidoscopic starlings picking away
at the mortar of the pharmacy and bank,
parking meter gulls on patrol overhead,
wandering trenchcoated babble-agents,
fast-walking knit-brow conspiracy hoarders
rolling cigarettes on Connecticut Avenue,
blue-grin cruisers in Kramers Books,
derelicts warm-dozing on platforms,
sweaty paperback-clutchers puckered up,
hyperventilating, prepared for onslaught,
as creatures of the underground fight it out
with glares for onlookers who witness it
all transpiring like television characters
dragging out the heart's deep treasures
on display for bored and weary citizens.

Babel

And what do you want to know?
Savage suck-up, greasy pike-puller,
lustful couples out to out-do each other,
sick weary children in hotel rooms?
You're quoting yourself at birth.

In this blunt enclave of civilization,
artifacts reign from lifetimes ago.
I'm here verily in seat 33 it seems,
sending out messages through nothing
you'll find in the scholar's notebook.

Word strands in DNA that never end,
street-arguing the aorta out of clench,
grip, sink and fall—siren, horse-clop,
humming illusion, bystander speculation,
hands reaching into pockets for money.

Where to, old pal? Rest your amendment?
Frenzy flight across mall and monuments
into the dusty wooden smell of offices?
Creep in the rain whip whizzing 'round
young couples careening towards a kiss?

Oh, you are a great sacrificial signer
of cramped footnotes and hidden scripts
on the way to the next stop after so much
bench-sitting and gallery line-standing
to catch a glimpse of the holy fire.

A Cold Clean Skeleton

Cancel connect—
rain weary coders neglect their charges,
shelter instead inside bars and cackle,
a few drinks in and I'll out annunciate you!
Obfuscate and scry—
in the street battle, love, a test of wills,
who gives in, the submissive one,
will take on all our sins...

Into the white marble skull theater
I stumble—you have your agenda:
done by 9, out by darkness when
streets are home to shadows only,
patrolling for an offering...

Somewhere in the reading room,
echo of a boot falling into a well.
Hanging in space, the tired scholar
stares at ledger pages of unreadable
marginalia meaningful as leaf veins,
city arteries overlain in coincidental
harmony so that Pennsylvania Avenue
leads us back to the spring of life...

Welcome, Potomac, dirty secret
river of dread commerce, I surrender
my coins for a stroll. Shallow backwash,
shaker possessed of deep-sea urgency,
lifetime cries heavy as Marley chains,
what river will wash you, shrive you,
St. Judas? Lincoln in his depression cage,
Roosevelt rising from his iron chair,
the convicts' melancholy emperor?

Every street is a microcosm of great vision,
exile in the madhouse, asleep at the wheel,
drunk on the putting green, propped up
in press conferences and hungry for a score,

tick-like and animated by electrodes
long after Elvis has left the building.

Sausages, cigarettes, bare-knuckle fighters,
the squint-witness drowse of an old horse,
and who will make it to a postage stamp?
Bull feathers! Bearded lizards!
The navy takes all comers—make-shift
Zen-posturing—did I catch you off guard?
Up for a drink? Who has the constitution?

In Thomas Cole's "Journey of Life"
the river running through youth years
curves off from the shimmering temple dome,
with young man confident at the helm—
but if you look closely, you'll see a little
footpath leading off from the river
towards the gleaming city beyond…

The sound of the river, lulling sad
ego-familiar strain the dead hear
after mourners have drifted on—
testament rising thought by thought,
a brain cathedral, another grand gaol
that the sweet white angel draws us into
with comfort-hand stabbing another
heart into the chest to rend, to mend…

Now night unfolds its rippled tents,
and wind arrives full of augments,
far shore surrogates crawling across
continents and inland settlements—
I sing to thee from cool airy terminals,
opal vales, the time has come to rise
from the blue home of troubled sleep
and cruise the warm indulgent seas
that surge and rock for you and me…

Breaking the Roof

The street articulates its warren run,
animal cry, its hustle and feral eye,
beauty on parade, imago mundi,
you parasitic pompous ass—yes you,
fake Buddha with your fist raised,
the common man you secretly disdain—
freedom for all as long as you're paid.
Market thieves will get you. They always do…

Sink sad plebe, cousin of dubious intent.
We circle each other like alpha wolves
near fresh meat, the universe in a nutshell:
look for it in clocks, plotlines, bus routes,
grocery aisles, philosopher illuminations,
in the empty air, blue in the face,
with friends vainly trying to resuscitate…

They're gathering at Dupont Circle
with flags and banners and little fires,
heading up Connecticut to the White House,
crawling through lizards of revolution.

Who is the dilettante lured by P Street,
heading west with a quiet seducing call
dissolving step by step, incipient neighbors,
to fluctuating gangplanks up to rocking
boatloads of wonder-blanched faces?

A Man Searching

Him off to work
        and new wife arriving
marble thighs
        secret messages left
in the stony crevices
        out in the grove
her mephitic thoughts
        and a luring kiss
whisper in the ear
        I'll come for you
carrying throughout the day
        a terrible blush

Give me your tired
        eyes sad for delivery
in these corridors
        far from light and air
conduits wet visceral hanging
        bloated from ceilings
the strum and strang of machine
        wheels and pistons
working away behind
        hot voluptuous walls
with guards at the gate
        for search and seizure
and windows through which
        we'll never pass

Freeways that exit
        into swift connecting
access roads
        to little footpaths
on the shore by the sea
        and now this hideous
stigma of fecundity
        the winter wind
and trees along the dark
        thoroughfare

night rain falling
>	like unbound hair

An old cheap hotel
>	of mute cataract windows
and jelly roll tunes
>	on ancient radios
and time warp figures
>	in elongated elevators
blind eyewitnesses
>	to the street play

Ford Theater gloomy lit
>	white and sepulchral
open as a skull
>	we slide into
on Tenth Street above E
>	the eyes still peering
into the heart
>	of the shooting

Garden-rich flaneurial displays
>	and filigree subways under foot
with cankered countenances
>	and reflecting pools
elephant clouds unhinged and free
>	in equatorial paradise
yet no sage can dream
>	such beauty as a fool

The ghost city
>	loaded with cut-outs
and everywhere you turn
>	you are reminded
the dead outnumber the living
>	granite people
with embedded maps in mind
>	geometry of cruelty and grace
we harvest the stars
>	for gold in the axis

IV

Cape Blanco Suite: The Dark Road Diaries

"Wandering in open country is naturally depressing, and the interventions of chance are poorer there than anywhere else."
—Guy Debord

Progress

I flew out of Seattle fast,
into sleet and kick-up spray
on the road through the wreckage,
watery world, towns without names,
moments like vipers in the brain.
Where are you now, beautiful friend?

I drove through Portland in a storm
and barely saw it.

Midway on This Journey

The road, the interstate, broken
out of the fragments of constructs
and something from the wilderness.

Contraptions of madness in Woodburn.
Dusk and the empty way station.
Christmas Carols and crowds at Denny's—
I don't expect an answer.

Salem into darkness, needle on red,
a thousand faces in the rain.
Pick a room, choose an incarnation,
reading memoirs by the afflicted.

No Answer

Vehicles pass more like sound than substance.
A good foot of snow came down in the last hour.
Somewhere across the border of the dream-guard.
Hiss from the mountain, silence from the sky.
Everything we were is sheer as a cold exhale.

Umpqua

Towns arrive indelible as ideas,
with longing human voices
in the forests of wandering.
Sudden river, I almost forgot
your secret, fierce drive
through stone electric green,
the crows emerging
from grey vales, yet imagine.

Reedsport

From this bridge the suicides leap
on golden days like this—
and where their cries fade out
above the slow-going ships,
their souls go straight as rays
through the heart of the horizon.

Cape Blanco

Disappearing shore and the disappearing man—
I realize I'm becoming the engine that I drive,
and the road narrows down until no road at all,
just a dirt trail through a black pine grove,
to the disappearing shore where the waves roll
and distance is a white flare from the edge
then gone with a green mist sliding in
obliterating everything except for one lighthouse
stabbing its fierce light for the wandering souls
and seabirds cruising in from the dark.

The Lighthouse Keeper

In this season he knows
we are smaller than wind,
as the storm blast sings
through the boarded glass.

He opens his door
to the sting and stab of rain,
making his leaning way
under the arc-lamp light.

In the radio house he listens
as distress codes come,
and he relays their signals
upland in obliterating wind.

No one can help them.
He can't respond but by prayer
and the light he throws
to every soul out there.

Morphic Zen in Oregon

Delay, engine trouble, hopefully a quick fix.
What lesson is embedded here? Once
on the way with Sharon at the wheel,
either heading to or away from home—
Seattle was home and Berkeley was "away."

Enough time passes, gradually it blurs.
Either direction leaves a self behind,
an invisible hand, anxiety of road time,
the same darkness on either side,
circling back, the next storm coming in.

Stuck in Medford

Sometimes the gods give you
just what you ask for.
Yet behind their venomous blessings
the out-bound train shudders.
The apartment rattles, windows shake,
the silence is always the same—

The black river rolls through town,
the black river flows under tower bridge,
the black river slides through hold-ups,
hide-outs and shooting stars—
carries us one and the same,
naked and strange to beautiful shores.

Newborn with another chance,
realize, it was never over.
The stars are the teeth of Buddha.
Choose your dream.
Choose the song of your life.
Leap into the firelight,
creature born of sweet delight.

Revelation

There are worse things than being alone.
Even in a town like this, between passes,
snow-laden, barred from my destination,
so I thought, so I thought.

The faces—bad teeth, ancient eyes—
people walking slow grey streets,
night music, bars loaded till two,
scattering moths in morning light.

Report

Made it through the pass unscathed—
through snow, the valley, across the plateau—
got chased by the highway patrol—
Hid out in a rest stop outside of Redding.

I don't know if there is enough road.
I don't know if there is enough road
before the next re-entry.

I just keep driving,
yeah, I keep driving.
I drive—

California Road

Live oaks clustered in arroyos,
a hawk in glide circles above,
hills like waves on the ocean itself:
I've plundered this road before...

Miles are memory, the trips of a child
in the battery acid haze-taste,
the heat, one more stop, one more town—
Eureka, Crescent City, a motel room
where we smuggle in the dog, watch TV,
swim in the greasy pool, see it as fun,
not the lost apartment off Telegraph,
the beating drums of People's Park,
sleepers in the doorways, music,
streets and sirens neverending...

As I drive through Ukiah, I see
an old woman burned dark as oak
drinking in the courthouse garden
throw her empty bottle down,
another day beneath the double light.
Wings unfold from her shadow.

Awake in anonymous motel room,
white walls, bloodstained sinks,
a blue handprint on the pillowcase,
earmarked pages in a Gideon Bible,
a phone that never rings...
nothing lonelier than being sick,
alone, in a motel room.
A long and disturbing silence,
not even wind. Then, unnatural scraping
on the wall outside, slowly diminishing,
feral, malevolent.

80 to the Bay

Allendale, the return of signals,
talk shows about becoming a cop,
(take the test until you pass.)
Vacaville with Manson in his hole.
R&B, Earth Wind and Fire…
the green hills part to reveal the bay,
Great America, a date with Traci Crough,
Hilltop Mall, Hercule and Pinole,
Kfog, El Cerito—now I'm the ghost
vehicle heading up University Avenue,
past the UC Theater and West Campus
still vibrating with eternal sorrows.
The liquor store is now a Montessori.
Andronicoh's is faded but extant.
La Tolteca is long gone.

Looking through Time's Eye

The dead ivy on that rooftop is a fire hazard—
you better strip off all those tongues,
the great combining engine gearing down
into your hands, the plan working itself out
and all lined up on shelves in Moe's
where I'm flipping through a Kafka book,
back from The City with a six pack of Kirin,
up to Lake DeAnza, evening sun in the trees,
John Clark's dog chasing a deer into the reeds,
evening Carrie slipping naked into the creek,
water over shoulders stroked by moonlight,
and through the big window on LeConte
the hillside is loaded with green Myazaki
creatures unashamed of their animation,
squirrels bickering about forgotten seeds
with their angry little flower overlords,
crows hunched above the Buddha garden,
and the alleyway basketball hoop still ringing
from a shot you made when no one was looking.

Hallucination in a Rearview Mirror

Berkeley to Seattle non-stop, I imagine
straight through clean and clear, speed
unknown, childhood days on this same route,
white-out heat-blanched highway out of
Arbuckle to Corning, distance nothing but silver
shimmering road writhing before and after,
briefly, then seemingly vanished completely.
In Red Bluff old signs of life in the live oaks;
Battle Creek, a coat fluttering on a wire fence.
And it begins, the first wave of the Siskiyous,
beautiful blue Lake Shasta like a dreaming crab,
island eyes into Whiskeytown undiminished,
Weed and the winter I wandered into a field
glittering with snow and world-sinking sadness—
it seemed all rivers flowed from the north.
Now driving those days I thought long gone
wash through like a fever-break in Yreka,
on the border, relief of Ashland at night,
thinking I'm free, from Medford to Salem,
then surprise as I break through Portland,
black waters, gleaming bridges, interstate
through flatlands flooded with moonlight.

Rivers

"Nothing is ever lost, sir. That is the beauty of a river view."
—Mr. Chagla, A River Sutra

There are rivers we find, unexpected,
driving out of the long golden hills,
wide, as though direct from the forge,
respected in distance by small communities.
And there are hidden rivers marked only
by dry riverbeds left where they ran,
vaporous shadows, hints of water that was
and the water we pray will come again.
Then there are secret rivers not on any map,
on the go even when we think they're still,
flowing unseen, unfelt as we flow with them.

Roadside Sideshow

Wild rides, crowds,
music from the stages,
gardens full of food,
animals in cages,
laughter, screams of terror,
gondolas rocking overhead—
the sun descends,
and above all
the ferris wheel spins
with souls swimming out
in the dreamsea night.

Let's Take This Moment to Consider

The road unfolds under my headlights.
The river is flowing somewhere near.
Homes appear out of darkness
blazing in groves then falling away,
poplars feathered under warp clouds
high-stepping across the world.

The road goes through nothing,
and I think nothing for the duration.
A station flutters Delta Dawn,
then back again to humming engine
and thoughtless drone between worlds,
the feel of the river I know is near,
illuminated by occasional moonlight
when the wind tears the clouds apart.

I Keep Looking for Myself

"I am cruising because I have dedicated myself to all that is creative and destructive in my life right now...and I am in love with the frantic chaos of this limitless universe."
—Timothy "Speed" Levitch, *The Cruise*

in flashback loops going back to Virginia
and the mathematician's madhouse in the hills,
the stark statement of a Hemingway sentence
in my head honed down to the bone to describe
a moment on Cal campus when I walked holy
morning light through the eucalyptus grove
and knew fleeting as my joy was it was a true
glimpse of the fire I'd seek forever—
set on my path, hook or by crook, to find
the magic word to crack the head wide open
like those party balloons drifting over
the Greek Theater, Grateful Dead music
moving like smoke through serpent streets—
driving Winthrop, looking for Delancy Ridge
and Last Chance Point, a place I think I came to
a lifetime ago and broke, ragged, agitated,
a shadow in the firelight twitching with anxiety
and between-world confusion with a monster
nemesis in the pine grove staring me down,
jolting the third eye to waking in wonder
with a white-tail deer across the clearing—
blow a kiss to the old self after the wave-hits
and we emerge with the ah, now I get it,
rocky saw-tooth, pine-scrabble launch point
and landing base for return-to-earth and us,
the ones who journey down the magic roads.

V

Eternal Return

"In the 'possible rendezvous,' on the other hand, the element of exploration is minimal in comparison with that of behavioral disorientation."
—Guy Debord

The Divine City

"Lead, kindly light, lead thou me on;
the night is dark and I am far from home."

I feel my way as if blind,
though I am not blind.
Simply, I hunger to see outside of time
through the spell of your eyes again,
to witness again how to drift awake
Broadway beholding in your company
the hieroglyphic brass dance steps
and a street that's paved with words,
the flag snapping over the bank
like the flame of your hair,
reflections in these windows that roll
like the current of a river.

Everything is diminished by your silence.
The light dims.
Even the beggars lose their sense
that an offering will come.
The books at Twice Sold Tales
have the drab look of old bones.
When the bus passes
there is no music in its engine.
The birds are naked with worry,
and their songs are no celebration.

I approach the gold window
the way a dead man rises to his god.
Sounds of traffic cannot distract me.
Shapes flow from the smoke
rising out of the funeral home.
I occupy the shadow of the lamppost.
The El Capitan Apartment bears the black
letters of its name across a yellow wall,
and I circle it as if it were a talisman,
secret charm to the mystery mountain.

The cat that moves soft as silk,
the acolyte, the witness
to your objects and rituals.
The bathroom sink with one
handle locked in place,
the book open, everburning lamp;
each step, each glance,
the choosing of a coat to wear
are all varied stations of grace.

In what street will you appear?
Everything is punished by your absence.
And if I should approach by prayer,
who would hear me?
I thought I caught a glimpse of you,
and followed that apparition through
the sunlit and the shaded avenues,
elusive shape flickering just
beyond the reach of my call,
until I broke into a run
and winning near found not you
but another bewildered stranger.

You see that could be me
muttering in the street, filthy, lost,
a wandering monster to everyone;
could be me laughing for no reason
then timid at the bus stop;
could be me buried in a book
or wracked by a hangover;
bound in a classroom, stark in the mortuary,
smoking in a theater door;
and it could be me at night alone
counting sirens and screams,
by the lake where lovers lie
listening to seaplanes rise.

I feel my way through
the crowds only alive
by a chance you might emerge.
I return to your window at night
with a green jewel ache in my chest.
What offering, what sacrifice
can I make? Talk and talk
and that lock never open. I reach
like a drowning man for the sun.

I strike through black.
The moon has one offer, gives
one light through the empty foyer.
A fierce intuition guides me,
one way up the turning stairs.
It has taken lifetimes to arrive,
to hack away the syntax of things.
Blessings to sighs and crows that jeer,
blessings to the nightmare dwellers
and to their faces carved by fear,
blessings to the honest drunk
who weeps among the accident flares,
and blessings to the one
I cannot see but know is there.

ACKNOWLEDGMENTS

"Investigation of the Spectacle," *Abandon Journal*
"Lighthouse Keeper," *Acumen*
"Ghost Town", *Cargo Literary Journal*
"Dupont Circle," "No Answer," *Descant*
"Preface," "Spokane Falls at Dawn," "Epilogue," *Dodging the Rain*
"Derive, A Drift," *Eastern Iowa Review*
"Empty Houses Ring," *Filling Station Magazine*
"Cape Blanco," *The Inflectionist*
"Mortality of Film," *JMWW*
"Smoke and Mirrors," *Lines + Stars*.
"Ghost Town," *Lost River*
"Brocken's Specter at Shady Grove," "Ouroboros," "The Library," *North of Oxford*
"Riding out the Night Listening to Comedians," *The Pedestal*
"The Divine City," *Penumbra*
"Dupont Circle South," *Pine Row*
"The Road," *Plato's Cave*
"Derive with a Buddhist Monk," *Poetry East*
"Umpqua," "No Answer," *Random Sample Review*
"Empty Houses Ring," *The Rumpus*
"Rivers," *Sand Hills Literary Magazine*
"The West Door," *Scrawl Space*
"Dupont Circle South," *The Stillwater Review*
"Place is the House of Being," *Banyan Review, Tipton Poetry Review*
"The Empty City" *Two Cities Review*

Special thanks to a CCHA Fellowship on American Cities and Public Spaces. Their support allowed me to explore Washington DC in all its seasons and to access the Library of Congress special holdings. Much of this work would not have been possible without their generous support.

Douglas Cole has published eight poetry collections, including *The Cabin at the End of the World*, winner the Best Poetry Award in the American Book Fest, and the novel *The White Field,* winner of the American Fiction Award. His work has appeared in journals such as *Beloit Poetry, Fiction International, Valpariaso, The Gallway Review* and *Two Hawks Quarterly*. He contributes a regular column, "Trading Fours," to the magazine, *Jerry Jazz Musician*. He also edits the American Writers section of *Read Carpet*, a journal of international writing produced in Columbia. In addition to the American Fiction Award, his screenplay of *The White Field* won Best Unproduced Screenplay award in the Elegant Film Festival. He has been awarded the Leslie Hunt Memorial prize in poetry, the Best of Poetry Award from Clapboard House, First Prize in the "Picture Worth 500 Words" from *Tattoo Highway*, and the Editors' Choice Award in fiction by *RiverSedge*. He has been nominated Six times for a Pushcart and Eight times for Best of the Net. His website is https://douglastcole.com.

www.ingramcontent.com/pod-product-compliance
Lightning Source LLC
Chambersburg PA
CBHW020337170426
43200CB00006B/421